My Wife Has Joined The Pink Bubble

What Do I Do Now?

Andy Stirrat

The author wishes to express a special thanks to James (ACE) Alexander for his
Awesome Illustrations that grace the cover and interior of this publication.

Disclaimer

DEDICATION

To the Men of Mary Kay whether you be Husband, Boyfriend, Dad, Brother or a "Wanna Be…" I hope you find this resource helpful.

CONTENTS

ACKNOWLEDGMENTS

My heartfelt and grateful appreciation to my Mary Kay "Daddy," Rob Langford and to the many other husbands of National Sales Directors and Top Sales Directors who have shared unselfishly with me. Most of all, thanks you to my wife Marsha who does this business with a poise and grace that makes me want to be the best "Mary Kay Husband" ever.

1 Introduction

"God first, family second, career third."
~Mary Kay Ash

  This business is different from any other I have experienced. It has its own culture, its own set of priorities and a unique value system in the secular business world. It has a unique legacy, has operated successfully for over 50 years and is debt free.

  In a world where businesses are shrinking, downsizing and "waiting for a better environment," Mary Kay is growing domestically and globally, continuing to introduce new and innovative products and making record profits. I find it amazing that as the economy has worsened, Mary Kay has continued to increase the compensation plan, their legacy car program and the rewards for top performers.

  Mary Kay Cosmetics offers an incredible opportunity to families today. The Founder, Mary Kay Ash, originally set out to write a book for women on how to survive in a business world dominated by men. What she ended up creating was an incredible business plan that is specifically designed to help women keep the priorities of God first, Family second and Career third. By maintaining these priorities, every woman has the opportunity to become a better Christian, Wife, Mother and Friend, while becoming as successful as she desires. Relying on "Golden Rule" thinking, Mary Kay built a company that with little of no advertising is one of the most recognized brands in the world today. One of Mary Kay's favorite sayings was "if you want to get the word out, don't telephone or telegraph, just tell a woman." Even considering the way we communicate today via text, twitter or Facebook, telling a woman is still the basic sales model.

Mary Kay made a special effort to create an opportunity that could be easily adapted into a woman's busy life and provide a maximum income for her efforts. She can choose between working in her own home or in the homes of clients or hostesses. She can choose whether or not she stocks inventory and if so how much. She chooses when to work based on her current lifestyle.

Mary Kay wisely recognized that women have an advantage over us when it comes to building relationships, nurturing and providing emotional support. These skills are intuitive for women, possibly a part of their motherly instinct but that is a guess on my part. What is apparent is that Mary Kay had the vision back in 1963 that businesses are just now beginning to appreciate today - women make great coaches, work well on teams and are able to connect with other women on an emotional level. These abilities enable them to build relationships with customers, encourage some of those customers to join their team and lead them to success.

One of the most incredible aspects of the company culture is the positive enthusiasm that these ladies generate. My personal feeling is that this aspect is more valuable than the money or cars that can be earned, the trips that can be won or the diamonds they can receive for doing their jobs. Attend any Mary Kay event and you will feel this infectious enthusiasm.

The first question many men ask when their wife embarks on the Mary Kay journey is what will my wife be doing? In a nutshell, she will be learning how to retail products from a top-selling brand of skin care and cosmetics with over 50 years of experience to share. In a recent study on Brand Recognition, Mary Kay was up there with Google, Avis and Coca Cola for brand recognition - a strong indication of Mary Kay's dominance and leadership in their industry.

In the beginning, your wife will learn a lot about the products, how they are used, how to determine skin types and tones, how to work with customers and how to develop a clientele. The training is freely provided by her Sales Director and her peers, often in a weekly sales meeting. The person who brought her into the Mary Kay opportunity or her Director will probably invite her to watch them do some appointments and may even attend your wife's first appointments to help her build confidence and skills.

As she builds her clientele, some of her customers will want to hear about the opportunity and perhaps join your wife's team. Once again, Your wife's Director or someone who has been in the business for a while will help her with her first few interviews to help her gain some confidence with sharing the business opportunity.

Mary Kay was very wise when she first developed her business plan. There are no territories assigned to Consultants nor are there quotas that have to be met. Mary Kay knew that this business would thrive on personal relationship selling and therefore, a Consultant might add a team member that lived in another town, perhaps even a different state. She envisioned an Adoptee Sales Director program which is still unique in the direct selling world today. That program guarantees that no matter where a Consultant is, she can attend a success meeting and have the help and mentoring from a Director that is local to her and she can expect to be treated as a member of her adopted unit even though that Director will never receive a dime of commission for her efforts. Before you start worrying about that Director, let me assure you that Director probably has team members that are being supported by other adoptive Sales Directors around the nation. This program enables someone to literally grow their business anywhere in the country. This also allows your wife the flexibility to move about the country should the need arise and still be able to find a supportive meeting and encouraging Director wherever she is.

In addition to teaching women how to share about skin care, how to look and feel beautiful and how they can make extra money, your wife will also begin servicing her customers. A fascinating thing happens every evening when Mary Kay customers go to bed at night. They wash their products off and reapply them the following day. This is a consumable product and part of the training involves keeping customers for life. Reorders make up a significant portion of a Consultants income and if she continues to increase her customer base, she will continue to raise this residual income each year she is in business.

Another Question you will probably have is where will she be doing this work? The answer to this actually boils down to individual choice. Mary Kay allows the Consultant to choose between meeting her clients in their homes or in her own home. As an independent business owner, she will also have the option to work whatever hours suit her schedule. My suggestion is you both sit down with a weekly plan sheet once a week and determine what works best for your family. She has no minimum hourly requirement but she also has no upside limit on her earnings - the more she can work, the higher her income potential.

One of the things that my wife has managed to do incredibly well is fit this business into her everyday life. When she goes to the grocery store, post office, bank or any of the many things that go into being a mom and a wife, she meets people that become her customers. We can be eating at a restaurant and she will offer the waitress a complimentary facial. When we attend functions in our community, meet with friends and just do life, we are often delivering products that have been ordered off Marsha's web site or an email, phone or text message.

The Mary Kay Web Site is probably our greatest income producing asset besides the parties and facials Marsha does. Mary Kay provides a professional web presence for Consultants for a very modest fee. At this writing, it is $60 per year plus tax and they offer it at half price to new Consultants. The company maintains it and keeps fresh and exciting. Other direct selling opportunities charge that or more per month and require the user to do much of their own maintenance.

Typically Marsha will see her customers several times per year so she can show them new products and make adjustments to their skin care regimen based on season and life changes. Her customers often reorder their products from her website at their convenience. I was once told by a business mentor that the money you earn while you are sleeping will make you rich. We are not rich by any means but we are very comfortable with the money Marsha's website brings in while we are awake and asleep!

I am sure that there are some of you reading this right now and thinking - I am a little concerned about what changes I may see in my wife. I can totally assure you that Mary Kay's life and business philosophy revolved around the priorities of God first, family second and career third. Your wife will become a better wife and mother for having spent time with other women who have chosen to set their life path under this same philosophy.

If you haven't already done so, now would be a great time to sit down with your wife and begin planning and dreaming together. I am exited about the future you will share!

2 My I - Story

"The Lord said, 'It is not good for the man to be alone. I will make a helper suitable for him."
~Genesis 2:18

"Mary Kay eloquently reminds us the only way to successfully manage all areas of our lives is to have our values and priorities in place."
~Roger Staubach Former Dallas Cowboy Quarterback

One of the very first things a new Mary Kay Consultant is taught and encouraged to do is to share her "I-story" at her Mary Kay parties and appointments. It is basically a short version of who I was and what I thought before I encountered this business opportunity, what I have leaned and accomplished and how it has changed my life. Here then is my I-story:

My first experience with Mary Kay came when my wife Marsha asked if I would be supportive of her should she make Mary Kay her career. She had been a Mary Kay Consultant for quite a while before we met but never had the ability to throw her heart over the bar and make a real attempt at becoming a top Director.

I am not ashamed to admit that at the time, I knew nothing about the company nor did I have a clue about how much money women spent keeping their skin soft and beautiful. I mistakenly thought it was all about lipstick and could not imagine anyone selling enough lipstick to make it worth their time much less earn the use of a free car.

We had both been in previous marriages and we were in the process of blending/reconciling our children as a family. I brought 4 teenagers into the family, Marsha blessed us with a teenager and 2 elementary age children. I really felt that Marsha did not need to be working outside the home as our schedule revolved around the activities and needs of our children and I was making enough to support us.

Fortunately, Marsha is just a little more stubborn than I am or maybe I just really cared about her being happy - either way she became a full time Mary Kay Consultant.

At the time, I was working 7 days a week for a major auto manufacturer. I was bringing home great income but enjoyed very little family time. One of the things we were passionate about was the desire to attend church together as a family. Marsha suggested that once she was earning enough from her Mary Kay business, perhaps I could stop working Sundays so we could attend church. Now Sunday was double overtime - I agreed, figuring it might take a year or two for her to reach that level. On her very first party, she made more in 2 hours on a Saturday afternoon than I did working all day Sunday. About a month after she started, I quit working Sundays and started regular attendance at church with my family.

A short time later, we realized that I really did not need to work Saturdays either. There were some adjustments that had to be made as most of her parties and meetings were in the evenings but I did get to spend some real quality time with the kids at Soccer practice, Band practice, Drill Team and Cheer Leading practice. Did I mention that between us, we have 7 children? I did a lot of driving... some cooking.... lots of homework.

Before the end of her first year in business, I had quit letting my company buy back my vacation days and I was using them for what they were intended. One of the most interesting aspects of taking vacation days was watching Marsha make money even while we were playing. As I have mentioned, women wash their makeup and skin care products off every night and therefore need to repurchase it on a regular basis. More often than not, Marsha would leave product on our porch for them and they would leave a check - Awesome!

As Marsha grew her business, earned her red jacket, picked up her first free car on her way to becoming a Director, she started asking me to attend her Mary Kay events and meetings. I went to a Seminar banquet and met her Director and some of her friends. I remember the genuine enthusiasm and positive encouragement everyone shared and felt like it would be great if my company treated me that way.

When Marsha was finishing Directorship, she asked me to be responsible for music and media at her meetings. I reluctantly agreed if she would purchase sound equipment, projector, laptop, microphones... She shared with me that she felt like a boom box would be sufficient but I held my ground. Thus began my involvement and commitment to her business. I would cart that equipment into our Monday night success meeting, set it up, play music and cart it home every week. When we first started, it would sometimes be Marsha, her guest, her assistant and me but we did it up proper every time.

I also began attending all her conferences, Seminar and training. I planned my vacations around our annual trip to Leadership, Career Conference and Advances (In Mary Kay we never retreat.) I found that the positive atmosphere helped me in my stressful corporate job.

The most incredible benefit I have received from being a Mary Kay husband is the personal growth in my spiritual walk of faith. I am constantly amazed at the progress I am seeing in that walk - particularly since my semi-retirement. I refer to it as a semi-retirement because I work just as much helping Marsha as I ever did working. The biggest difference for me is that instead of driving 45 minutes in rush hour traffic first thing in the morning, I spend my first hour in prayer and scripture reading with Our Lord and Savior. I did not realize how important this was until I had the ability to make it my priority. Thanks to Marsha's Mary Kay business, I am able to spend my most productive hour of the day praying for my family, my friends, our church, Marsha's team and our Nation. I love our Mary Kay business!

As Marsha's business grew, we began praying for me to be able to retire early so Marsha and I could work together and enjoy more quality time. Four years after she became a Director, My company offered me an early retirement. Most men would probably not leave a 6 figure income at age 52 with kids still in high school. I promise you I was not financially in a position to walk away from my steady paycheck. We prayed about it and realized we had been praying for something like this to happen in our lives. In faith, we decided this was the answer to our prayers - I took a reduced pension and left my job of 25 years. I would not have considered this move had it not been for this awesome business we had built and my faith in our ability to work together to grow it.

Since October of 2006, we have had the privilege of working together, eating just about every meal together and being able to spend quality time with our children and our children's children.

I am thankful for Mary Kay for providing our family with the financial security that allows us the quality of life we enjoy, but I am even more thankful for what it has done for Marsha as a wife and mother. Running her business under Mary Kay's priority of God first, family second and career third has helped to shape her into the precious wife and mother God intended her to be. Mary Kay's attention to the biblical Golden Rule philosophy of "do unto others as you would have them do unto you" coupled with the go-give attitude of the top leadership has helped her develop into the caring woman of poise she is today.

3 Marketing Structure

"First, let me assure you that this is not one of those shady pyramid schemes you've been hearing about. No sir. Our model is the trapezoid!"
~The Simpsons

With any business that relies on direct sales for promotion, there are certain words used to describe the structure of that business. Most companies use the Multilevel marketing approach in which there are multiple layers between the salesperson and the company. When someone joins one of these companies, they purchase their products through their sponsor which is the person who brought them into the company. The typical commission for someone starting out is lower and as they build a team, their combined orders bring that salesperson's discount up.

Mary Kay sells directly to the Consultant resulting in what the company refers to as a dual marketing system. The company sells directly to the Consultant who in turn, sells it directly to her customers. It does not matter how far up you are in the company nor does it matter how many members you have on your team, everyone receives the same discount on their product. Many men have asked me about Marsha's down-line, sponsor, up-line, sideline, and to be honest, I had to ask Marsha what they meant. Mary Kay shares some similarities to other direct sales companies but in many ways, Mary Kay is unique.

Mary Kay encourages Consultants to invite women to join their team. Consultants are part of a Unit that is lead by a Director. That Director may or may not have been the one to introduce that new Consultant into her Unit. Mary Kay provides a lucrative compensation to Director's to lead and train Consultants in her Unit regardless of who brought them into the company.

One of the most misunderstood aspects of the Mary Kay Business model has to do with Pyramid schemes. The loose definition of a Pyramid based business is that is a non-sustainable business that offers no product or service and involves the exchange of money - usually in the form of a sign-up. The only way to make money in a business such as this is by signing up new members whose sign-up fee pays the previous investors. These business schemes are illegal in every state and are pursued by the Federal trade Commission as well as the state Attorney General's office in the states they operate in.

Direct Sales companies are often confused with these business schemes because they reward their sales force for adding team members. Their similarities end there because a legitimate direct sales company offers a product or service that can be sold and provides income without signing up new members. In addition, members at any level can advance past the level of the person who signed them up. And it is worth mentioning, they are legal.

Companies often follow this marketing model to avoid the high cost of advertising. With more and more people opting for DVRs and services such as Netflix as well as reading internet versions of magazines and newspapers, word of mouth advertising makes more sense than ever. Fifty years ago, Mary Kay had enough wisdom to realize the very best way to promote her legacy was to provide incentives to her sales force to pass it on by word of mouth. Now Mary Kay corporate does invest modestly in various advertising media but it is highly targeted and gathers its success because it enhances the efforts of its direct sales force.

If you and your wife are considering this opportunity and this is a concern for you, I urge you to sit down with your wife's prospective Director and talk about these issues to help you have a feeling of assurance that this business is truly a legitimate opportunity. If her Director is out of town or can't meet on your schedule, you might consider a 3 way phone conversation or utilize Skype. Some questions you may want to discuss are:

> Will my wife be able to make money without signing up new team members?

> How will you help her find customers so she is not scaring off all of our friends and family?

In addition, ask for some company literature and some links to company videos and training materials. You will find that that Mary Kay does not promise you a get rich quick scheme. It does offer an opportunity to get paid well while having the flexibility to make choices about when to work, where to work and how much time will be devoted. The pay is proportionate to the time spent. I will tell you in all honesty, it will take work to build this business but it is well worth the effort.

The Starter Kit in Mary Kay is the only required upfront expense. The kit includes everything needed to demonstrate the product, samples to share with potential customers, brochures and learning tools such as a DVD and Consultants guide. The starter kit is $100 plus tax + shipping. The retail value of the kit and the bag that it comes in is estimated at over $400. In addition to a low startup cost, there is no inventory requirement although I suggest you consider talking with your wife and her Director about what the options might be. All inventory is backed by a one year 90% buyback from Mary Kay should your wife decide this business is not right for her.

Mary Kay will pay your wife a commission for orders submitted by anyone she brings into the company and I will cover more on that in a later chapter. I bring it up right now because I want to make sure you understand that team building is encouraged but one of the first things a Consultant should learn and get comfortable with is the sale of the product. Mary Kay provides the best products at a competitive price and when prospective customers try it, they are sold. I have watched it time and time again and it amazes me whenever I watch Marsha say: "Put some on - how does that feel? Now wipe it off - how does your skin feel? Want some?" The answer is almost always yes!

Mary Kay also provides satisfaction guarantee for customers. This means that when your wife sells a product to a customer, she can assure them that if they are not satisfied for any reason, they can return the product to her. Mary Kay takes all the risk here and will replace the product that your wife takes in return. This also helps your wife introduce new products to her customers because they get to try it out first. I can promise you that when a woman goes into a drugstore or department store and asks she can return her cosmetic products if she doesn't like them she will not have this same outcome.

Mary Kay envisioned a company that would allow women to continue being great mothers and wives while being able to earn an executive income with a flexible schedule. She had a unique understanding of direct selling from her own previous experience of being so successful in this type of marketing. Her unique vision centered on the nurturing nature of women. The nurturing starts with the Consultant/customer relationship. The goal in this relationship goes beyond simple selling of products. The ultimate reward for a Consultant comes from enabling her customers to feel good about the way they look and how they feel about themselves. I have heard many Consultants share stories of how they came to realization that through this process, they no longer viewed themselves as "in Mary Kay." They realized that Mary Kay was now "in them."

This nurturing concept is also enjoyed by the Consultant through the relationship she shares with her Director or an adoptive Director in her area. The nurturing relationship extends from Mary Kay directly to the Consultant also. This direct relationship allows the Consultant to take her concerns directly to the company and takes it out of the Multi Level Marketing model that most direct selling companies employ.

Mary Kay the company continues to invest in research to bring the best products for your wife to offer her customers. They are also providing innovative new ways to reach customers given the rapidly changing technological advances. I can assure you, as new developments arise, Mary Kay will be there to provide the support you and your wife will need to be amazingly successful in this business.

4 Success

"The real success of our personal lives and careers can best be measured by the relationships we have with the people most dear to us--our family, friends, and coworkers. If we fail in this aspect of our lives, no matter how vast our worldly possessions or how high on the corporate ladder we climb, we will have achieved very little."
~ *Mary Kay Ash*

"Every person is special! I sincerely believe this. Each of us wants to feel good about ourselves, but to me, it is just as important to make others feel the same way. Whenever I meet someone, I try to imagine him or her wearing an invisible sign that says: make me feel important! I respond to this sign immediately, and it works wonders."
~ *Mary Kay Ash*

When my wife Marsha first started attending her weekly success meeting with Mary Kay, I would say she was going to her Girl Cult. She urged me to accompany her to these meetings but I was unwilling take her business seriously. My only goal was to see she was happy. You know the cliché - "happy wife, happy life?" or how about "when Mom's happy, everyone else is happy?

I have radically changed my perspective on the "Girl Cult" thing and Marsha's happiness. As we have grown in our relationship, her happiness has become a much bigger priority than the old clichés might offer.

While Marsha gets a huge satisfaction from working and growing her business, she has also experienced some frustrations. Like any business or job for that matter, things do not always turn out as we plan. Appointments cancel, people don't always do what they say they will and let's face it - life happens. It has taken me a while to grasp this concept, but I have learned that when she is frustrated with her business, the very last thing she wants me to do is to try and help her "fix it." She has taught me that what she really wants is an encouraging word and some sympathy. It is a fundamental difference in how we as men view problems and how women share them.

One of the things I have learned about working with Marsha and her Mary Kay sisters is that women also share a different perspective on business than men.

While Success in sales, profit and business growth are important factors in any business, Mary Kay had the wisdom and foresight to build this business model based on women's needs.

While I am not an authority on the differences between men and women in business, I have noticed that women tend to be more focused on their relationships with their customers, team members and peers and place almost as much value on that measurement as they might the bottom line or profit margin. Where a man might ponder a business decision and share with his best friend, mentor or adviser what he has decided, a woman will make her decisions based on how her support group may feel about a given situation.

As men, we are often fortified with cash as an incentive and to an extent a measurement of our success. We work hard for bonuses and our paycheck is often a performance indicator for us. As long as the paychecks rise steadily, we are comfortable with our progress.
Please understand, I am not saying that women are not interested in bonuses, increasing their pay or making more money. I am suggesting that Mary Kay truly understood that women need to be

recognized and celebrated for what they do.

When you attend a Mary Kay meeting or event you will realize just how significant this is. Women are celebrated and recognized for absolutely everything they accomplish. "If you thought about selling something this past week, stand up and be recognized!" gets just as much woos, hollers and applause as "if you sold over $1000 in retail sales this week..."

One of the significant factors you will notice as you become immersed in "Girl Cult" is their definition of success. It would be easy to generalize and look at Mary Kay's most successful Sales Directors and National Sales Directors and focus on their fabulous earnings, prestigious cars and all expense paid trips and quantify those as their "why." Often they admit that is what attracted them to the business and helped them to stay on task to reach their objectives.

As you listen to these top performers teach and speak however you realize that is not part of their definition of success nor is it what they will recommend as a success strategy for your wife. Instead, they are focused on the differences it has made in the lives of the women they have touched and an overwhelming sense of gratitude that God has placed them in this position.

I can't tell you how many times I have heard a top National Sales Director say that once she allowed what she was doing to come into her heart, the money was not the motivating factor that kept her on track. I have heard Top National Sales Director Jill Moore say "Other than accepting Jesus Christ as my Lord and Savior, being a part of Mary Kay has been the single most important decision of my life and someone would have to yank it from my dead hands before I would give it up."

At Mary Kay guest events, you will often hear the speaker ask the audience "how many of you love your job so much you would go to work tomorrow even if you knew you would not receive any pay for it?" A look around the room will usually indicate all of the Mary Kay Consultants have their hands raised while none of the guests raise their hands.

This is not to infer that monetary need is not a motivator in the Mary Kay world. In fact, many top performers in the company came in to pay off a credit card, provide day care for their children, or just help their husband with their monthly financial obligations. Once immersed in the culture however, they came to the realization that Mary Kay the woman wanted so much more for them. She desired that every mom have the ability to raise her children without using day care and still earn executive pay. She wanted all women to feel special. In her teaching, she encouraged Consultants to imagine everyone they meet wearing a sign that says "make me feel important."

5 Feelings

"Taking joy in living is a woman's best cosmetic."
~ Rosalind Russell

"The reason women don't play football is because 11 of them would never wear the same outfit in public."
~ Phyllis Diller

There are plenty of great books on the differences between Men and women and how they deal with feelings so I will spend little time exploring these differences and just stick to some basics.

How we process our emotions is significantly different between men and women. While women tend to want to talk about their emotions, men are wired for action. As a result, we have a desire to fix anything that seems to upset our wives. When we sense our wife is discouraged in her business, we want to offer solutions or perhaps encourage her to quit.

When a man goes to work, his basic desire is to bring home money. That is not to say that men don't enjoy relationships with co-workers, being recognized for a job well done or the satisfaction that comes from helping others succeed and move up. It is just instilled in us from childhood that we work for money.

Men generally have a different style of relationship with other men such that they usually don't share feelings or place themselves in a vulnerable position with their co-workers. We are just built that way. Women on the other hand, enjoy a close circle of friends that they share with and are comfortable being vulnerable with. They share their hopes, fears, joys, sorrows and confidences and generally feel better for having that emotional support and being able to share.

We as men generally have our wives and perhaps a close buddy we share with and therefore may feel a little threatened when our wives become involved in a Mary Kay team. We may feel they are pulling away and seeming to get their happiness and emotional support from Mary Kay - perhaps even tying to become self-supporting and therefore no longer need us. Through the years, I have observed this thought pattern in fellow husbands and would like to share some perspective.

First and foremost, Mary Kay founded her company on biblical principals and therefore encourages the marriage relationship. She shared those values with the top leadership in the company and those values have not changed and I don't believe they ever will.

A significant aspect of being a privately owned debt-free company is the ability to stick by your beliefs and convictions. Mary Kay founded this company on Christian principles and had the foresight to leave her legacy in the hands of her Inner Circle of National Sales Directors and trusted family members to insure that the company never wavers from these beliefs.

6 Investment VS Debt

"In any investment, you expect to have fun and make money."
~Michael Jordan

"Rule No.1: Never lose money. Rule No.2: Never forget rule No.1."
~Warren Buffett

When I was much younger, I started a painting and remodeling business. I had worked as a painter, knew some carpentry and had friends proficient in the various remodeling trades. As I researched this business opportunity, I realized I would need a reliable truck to carry my equipment as well as myself and any crew I might hire. I signed a 48 month installment contract for a pickup and declared myself in business. I was interested in doing commercial work and quickly realized that in order to bid any jobs, I would have to show proof of insurance and workman's comp to hire a crew. I was able to purchase this with a considerable down payment and a monthly payment plan for the balance. Now I did have a few hand tools and ladders, drop cloths and other basic necessities but quickly realized I would need a lot more ladders drop cloths and tools to outfit a crew as well as invest in commercial spraying equipment.

Before I had lined up my first job, I had signed my name on the dotted line for over $20,000 in debt. Was I nervous? You bet I was. I had monthly living expenses to start with and now I had added business debt. Plus I had to quit a job that did not pay well but did provide a paycheck every Friday. Adding a crew of talented reliable workers also added a weekly obligation to provide a timely paycheck for these workers. This instantly made me aware of a need for working capital. I was fortunate in that early on I learned to request a deposit and periodic draw payments to see my contracts through completion. My business venture turned out successful and supported me and my family very well. I share this experience to help you see that any business requires planning, risk and investment.

I am not suggesting you go out and buy a new vehicle or anything else you don't need today to get started. What I am proposing is this:

Sit down with your wife and her Director and talk though the plan and any investment you will be making. Mary Kay uniquely helps with risk by offering a 90% buy-back policy of any unsold product within a year of purchase. That is huge when you consider that they cannot resell this product for obvious health and safety reasons as well as quality issues. They have no idea how this product was stored or whether it may have been tampered with and therefore must destroy any returned product. I just wish my 401k offered that same level of safety. I do not know of any other business venture or franchise that offers such a guarantee. Please understand - Mary Kay is not guaranteeing anyone's success in business. What they are saying is: We believe enough in our products to offer a 100% satisfaction guarantee to your customers and have enough confidence in the training and support you will receive to offer this opportunity with a safety net for you should it not meet your needs and expectations or perhaps more importantly, should your life circumstance change.

There is no cookie cutter formula for how much inventory a person needs to keep on hand. Mary Kay does not require inventory nor does it have a quota. It does have a minimal activity level to maintain the wholesale discount but it is totally up to the Consultant to determine how much business she wants to pursue.

In addition, at each level of inventory purchased when a Consultant starts her business and submits her very first order, the company provides free bonus product which can be resold at a profit. I am speculating here, but I believe the company offers this bonus product to offset any cost incurred in the order such as credit card or loan interest.

I am not ashamed to admit that when it came to stocking our shelves, I was a little concerned about how much we were committing ourselves to. We started out with what I now realize was a very modest investment but it seemed a lot at the time. Please understand, it was not a matter of whether I believed Marsha would be successful or not, I just did not realize the amazing potential Mary Kay offers.

Typically, a new Consultant will decide with her Director based on how much time and effort she anticipates investing in her business. Think of it like this: if you walk into a store wanting to purchase a pair of tennis shoes, your expectation is to walk out with some tennis shoes. The proprietor of that store wisely realized that if he did not stock your size in a variety of tennis shoes for you to choose from, you would leave his store and shop with a competitor.

Mary Kay is similar in that once your wife has encouraged someone to buy a particular product, that customer will want to take that product home and start using it right away. In addition, she will use that product daily and when she runs out, she will expect your wife to have it available for her. Another aspect is pure time spent. When Marsha goes to an appointment or someone comes to our house and purchases some product, it is much more efficient for her to hand that product to her customer at that moment rather than having to drive across town to deliver it later.

Having shared that, I do want you to know that if you and your wife decide it is not possible to purchase inventory, many Consultants run their business by accumulating orders and placing an order for products as they are needed. The best way to determine what works for your family is to sit down with your wife and figure out what her goals are for this business and what available resources you may have to work with. I have watched many Consultants start with nothing and build a substantial inventory in this way by reinvesting profits each time they order.

I am sure by now you are thinking "I thought we were getting into this to make money, not spend it." And you are right - that is exactly why you should be a part of the discussion with your wife and her Director regarding inventory. Even if your wife has been working this business for a while, it is a good idea to revisit this from time to time.

The most important thing I want to convey to you is that this business will work best for you and your family if you can reach a decision about inventory that you are both happy with so your wife can focus her working effort on building a successful business and servicing her customers in a way that is satisfactory to them.

Ways to fund Inventory

A common question Consultants have shared with my wife Marsha and I is where do they find money to purchase inventory once they have determined that keeping inventory is their right choice based on business goals.

There are numerous ways to approach this, the most simple being a consumer credit card. Mary Kay accepts Master Card, Visa, Discover and American Express for product orders. Starting at profit level inventory means profit on every sale of the product so from the outset, your wife will be able to restock what she sells, service the loan obligation on her credit card and show a nice profit after each sales transaction.

Depending on your credit and your relationship with your banker, your bank may still offer lines of credit and signature loans. Banks often will offer a more favorable interest rate but be prepared with Credit reports, Tax statements and a business plan as they will require a little more in the way of security and perhaps collateral.

An overlooked source of funding might be found in the ability to borrow from a life insurance policy or against your 401k or other savings plan. I don't pretend to understand or know all the rules or tax law in this respect - I do advise looking carefully at this option to make sure you are on solid legal standing.

Another place to seek business financing might be in those friends and family member who love and believe in you. I have seen Consultants borrow small amounts from several relatives enabling them to get started. Do not overlook holding a garage sale or using Craigslist or EBay to sell some unwanted items and infuse some cash into your startup.

Regardless of whether you borrow the funds or dig into your nest egg, Mary Kay still backs up the purchase of inventory with 90% buyback within a year of purchase. They know you are taking a risk in starting a business but this is their way of saying they will take on the bigger part of the risk. They know that if your wife will make an honest effort to share this product and opportunity with others, she will enjoy a successful business venture.

By keeping an inventory, your wife will sell more because women tend to buy on impulse but will want it right away. When her customer takes the product home after being introduced to it and shown its proper use, she will remember the application tips your wife shared because it is still fresh in her mind. In addition, your wife will enjoy a better dollar per hour wage if she is showing, selling and delivering in one visit rather than show and sell and return to deliver. It is also easier to hand the product to the customer and asks for payment than it is to say "pay me for the product and I will bring it to you later."

One final reason I would urge you and your wife to take a serious look at determining the best inventory level and maintaining it is that you and your family will then treat this business as a serious business and not a hobby. Knowing she can generate a profit any time she chooses, will give your wife confidence and motivation to get new customers and expand her business.

One other note to consider; Consultants who do not carry inventory are more likely to get frustrated and quit than those who stock inventory. By the same token, customers are more likely to stay loyal to someone who can provide what they need when they need it than from a Consultant who says "wait until I get a few more orders..."

Summing it up, I suspect you might be asking where will we keep this entire inventory? Cosmetics typically have a very small footprint. When Marsha first started, we inventoried several thousand dollars worth of inventory on two inexpensive snap together bookshelves I purchased at Home Depot.

7 Show Me the Money

"Leaders teach. They motivate. They care. Leaders make sure that the way to success is always broad enough and straight enough for others to follow."
~ *Mary Kay Ash*

This is one of my FAVORITE parts of the Mary Kay opportunity and being a Man, fits with my desire to follow the "bottom line." I am going to attempt to unpack this aspect for you so you will understand it and also to encourage you to help your wife to take advantage of everything that is available to her.

To start off with, Mary Kay pays one of the highest percentages in direct sales by allowing the Consultant to purchase product at a 50% discount. Every Consultant at every level of this business enjoys this 50% discount as long as they stay active with the company. This means that if your wife sells a $15 Mascara, she pockets $7.50 from the sale. That probably does not seem like a lot of money and really isn't when you look at as an individual item. When we look at it in the context of what women actually purchase to keep themselves young and beautiful looking, it is huge!

The average woman uses Cleanser, Moisturizer, some type of exfoliant, anti-aging wrinkle cream and eye cream on a daily basis. She puts it on and washes it off - daily. Some of it happens morning and night. She also uses make-up: foundation, concealer, mascara, eye-liner, eyebrow pencil, eye shadow, lipstick, lip-gloss, lip liners, blushers and perhaps a bronzer. Almost every day! And that is just on her face! On her body she uses shower gel, body lotion exfoliating scrub, nail polish, body spray and perfume.

It does not take long to realize that the average woman will spend somewhere in the neighborhood of $100 or more per month keeping her skin looking nice and healthy. If you figure a 50% commission and multiply that by 100 customers, that could become a significant amount of money.

That is just the beginning! Mary Kay's greatest wish was for her Consultants, Sales Directors and National Sales Directors to pass the opportunity on. It was her dying wish that in addition to helping women feel beautiful and therefore better about themselves, that they offer the opportunity to everyone they meet. When a Mary Kay Consultant shares the opportunity with her customers and someone joins her team, She becomes a Senior Consultant and the company pays a 4% commission for every wholesale order the new team member places. In many direct sales companies, you purchase from the person that brought you into the business. With Mary Kay, that is considered a serious "No-No" and could be cause for dismissal. Consultants buy directly from the company, therefore eliminating any confusion with pyramids and other schemes. In Mary Kay, you are either a Consultant purchasing your product at 50% wholesale or you are a customer buying at full retail from your beauty Consultant.

When your wife has added 3 new team members, she moves up to Star Team Builder status. This is considered the first level of management in Mary Kay - think of it as an Assistant Manager Position. At this level, she is still earning her 50% on her personal sales to her customers and she is receiving a 4% commission check from Mary Kay for any wholesale orders her team is purchasing. She also is entitled to wear the coveted Red Jacket - a symbol that she is serious about building her team. This level often entitles her to special seating at meetings and many will look up to her for guidance and inspiration.

Starting with her fourth qualified team member the company will give her a $50 bonus for each qualified team member she adds. Qualified means the new team member orders $600 or more in the first two calendar months of her business.

As a Star Team Builder with 5 or more active team members she moves up to team leader status and things start really happening! First off she gets a raise from the company to either 9% or 13%. She is still earning her 50% commission on her personal sales, and she will receive a 9% commission on her team member's wholesale orders from the company. If she does at least $600 in wholesale orders herself and 5 or more of her team members order that month, she will receive a 13% commission check on her team member's wholesale orders from Mary Kay. That is the same as doubling or tripling her commission for basically the same level of activity - and it gets better! At this level she can also go on target for the first level of Mary Kay FREE Career Car. I will cover the Career Car Program in more detail in the next chapter.

When 8 or more team members have joined your wife's team, she is considered a Future Director with the Company. She will still receive her 50% commission on her sales, the 9% or 13% commission on her personal team and the $50 team building bonus for each new qualified team member. In addition, the company and her Director will begin grooming her for the prestigious position of Mary Kay Sales Director. At this level, she will be invited to attend special leadership training and functions and she will likely participate in delivering the training at her success meetings.

Once she has added 10 or more personal team members, your wife may submit for D.I.Q. That stands for Director in Qualification but is often interpreted as "Do It Quickly" or by us husbands as "Dinner's In Question." Do not worry guys, I have included a few life sustaining recipes for us cooking challenged guys in a later chapter of this book!

During her Qualification period, she will need to add 14 members to her future Unit. Once she has begun the company qualification however, every team member that her personal team adds counts for her Unit as well. Think of it like this - if 3 of her personal team members promote themselves to Star Team Builder (3 or more team members) She will be up to 19 Unit members. She only needs to add 5 more to finish since She counts as one of the 24 required for her team.

It is during this period of rapid growth that she will most likely qualify for her first Mary Kay Free Car - Currently the Chevrolet Cruz outfitted with On-Star and Sirius/XM Radio as well as power windows, locks, security, cruise control - everything you she will need to arrive safely and comfortably to her Mary Kay Parties. Go drive one - this is a seriously nice car and guess what - you can drive it too provided your wife is willing to share and put you on the insurance.

Speaking of insurance, Mary Kay pays a large percentage of the insurance on her free car. Your wife will contribute a small percentage of the insurance but you will never miss it because it is taken out of her commission check. The percentage will vary by state but is nominal.

There is an option to take a cash compensation instead of a free car so if for some reason the Mary Kay vehicle does not work for your family situation, your wife gets the equivalent money added to her check each month which you can use to pay an existing car note or other bills.

Once your wife has a team of 24 she has become a Mary Kay Independent Sales Director. In addition

Unit 10% Volume Bonus	
Monthly Wholesale Unit Production	Monthly Bonus
$4000—$4999	No Bonus
$5000—$5999	$500
$6000—$6999	$600
$9000—$9999	$900
$20,000—$20,999	$2000
$30,000—$30,999	$3000

to receiving a 50% commission on her personal sales and a 9% or 13% of her personal team's wholesale orders, she is now entitled to an additional 13% on her entire team (remember once she reached 10 on her team, she was able to count her teams team members as part of her Unit,) and a 10%/1000 bonus on her Unit's production of $5000 or more.

Let me take a moment to explain this because it is a little confusing. When her team does $4999 Wholesale production, there is no 10% bonus. When her team does $5000 in wholesale production there is a $500 bonus. At $5999 the 10% is still $500, at $6000 it is $600. There is no upper ceiling on how much production your wife's team can submit therefore no upper limit on what this commission might be. For additional clarification, see the chart reflecting Unit 10% Volume Bonus.

In addition, she now receives $100 for each new qualified personal team member she brings in and she can receive a $300 bonus for 3 new qualified Unit members or a $500 Bonus for 5 or more New Qualified Unit Members. She also will have the potential to receive a $500 Bonus per quarter for having 15 Stars on her team, UP TO $2000 annually in Wellness bonus and an additional $1000 Bonus each for excellence in her first 6 months of Directorship for being "On The Move ($15000 in Total Unit Wholesale Production and 3 New Qualified Personal Team Members), Fabulous 50s (She build her Unit to 50 In first 6 months as a Director) and Honors Society ($50000 in first 12 Months and 50 Active Unit Members.)

I know that is a lot of numbers so I am going to try and simplify it for you. I will make some assumptions for simplicities sake so I will point out that your wife may or may not experience these numbers. When she first begins her business, it may be difficult to achieve these results. There is a very good chance that by the time your wife is a Director, her results will be much higher.

The following story is an example of how a family might progress and benefit from this business. The characters and their results are fictional and by intent are conservative to avoid any unrealistic expectation on your part.

Tiffany enjoys being a mom of two great kids and a wife to her college sweetheart Chris. Raising Addison and Lily give her immense pleasure and fulfillment and she is ever so grateful that Chris has a job that supports them so well.

There are times she wishes she could go back to work - even if it is just part time. Chris is really a great provider and they live in a comfortable home. Tiffany worries that Chris doesn't get enough downtime from his job and he often works overtime to provide some of the nicer things in life. They have talked about taking a trip to Disney World next summer but their budget just doesn't stretch that far.

Whenever Tiffany has brought up the subject of her getting a part-time job or reentering the work force, they have both agreed that her priority right now while the girls are so young is to be home for them. In addition, day care for Lily and after school care for Addison would eat up a large portion of any money she would earn.

One of the ladies in Chris and Tiffany's small group at church invited Tiffany to attend a "Get Cute For A Cause" pampering session at her home and Tiffany agreed to attend. Once there, Beverly, an independent Mary Kay Consultant treated her and several other women to a complementary pampering facial where she learned all kinds of great stuff about caring for her skin. She liked the products and purchased a basic skin care set. Beverly explained that a percentage of her profits that evening would go towards providing free products to Moms of children with special needs.

Beverley asked Tiffany if she could come by one afternoon and explain the Mary Kay marketing plan to her - she felt Tiffany would be good at doing what she did. Tiffany told her it would be okay to come by her home the next afternoon, she would love to hear the marketing plan but that she did not envision working for a few years.

Of course you already know she signed up and became a brand new Independent Mary Kay Beauty Consultant. Chris was livid she signed up without consulting him. Chris had some legitimate concerns about what Tiffany was getting herself into - he knew someone at work whose wife had failed miserably at it. They argued about it but Chris could tell Tiffany really wanted to try it out. After a night of arguing, they agreed he would come home early on Monday evening so she could attend her success meeting.

Tiffany attended her meeting and met her Sales Director who invited her to come watch her do a party that Thursday. Chris really wasn't happy when she came home and told him he would get to spend some quality time with their girls that Thursday but he reluctantly agreed.

Tiffany watched her Director sell several hundred dollars in the space of a few hours that evening and was all the more convinced that with a profit of 50% she would do very well in this business. Her Sales Director encouraged her to set up a Party to kick off her new business. She also scheduled an appointment to come over and discuss Inventory with Tiffany and Chris on Saturday morning.

Tiffany was a little apprehensive about making an investment in product to launch her new business. They lived on a tight budget and she was already experiencing some pushback from Chris about possibly being away from him and their girls so much.

When Tiffany's Sales Director came to have the inventory talk Chris was reluctant to join in the conversation. Tiffany's Director asked him what he knew about the company and opportunity. It seems some of his coworkers had convinced him it was a pyramid and no one ever made any money selling lipstick. Tiffany's Director explained the difference between direct sales and pyramid schemes and assured him Tiffany would be working with a company that was debt free and successful for over 50 years. In addition, she explained about the free training Tiffany would receive and that she was not required to team build although she would probably want to.

Once she explained how the company offers a 90% buyback on product purchases within the year, he was comfortable with looking at the options. Tiffany, Chris and the Sales Director established that Tiffany would work no more than 10 - 15 hours per week. Given that level of activity, they were able to determine a modest inventory for her to stock and replenish as she sold it. Once Chris realized that given the level of order they placed, the company would provide free bonus product that once sold would more than service the interest they might pay if they used a credit card. They were able to purchase her inventory with a credit card and ordered it right away.

They scheduled her party for the following Saturday to give her plenty of time to invite guests and pre-profile them with her Director's help. Tiffany texted all the women in her small group and some of the moms she knew from Addison's class and a few of her friends from the neighborhood.

Not everyone responded to her initial text so she tried calling them. By mid week, 5 of her friends had agreed to come, 2 asked if they could come at another time as they were busy and a few either said no or did not respond. Her Director assured her that this was normal and provided some scripts for her to use when pre-profiling and coaching her guests.

Saturday came and 4 of her 5 guests showed up and Tiffany's Director helped her sell over $350 in product. Tiffany already had the product on hand and was able to fill their orders. In addition, one of her guests felt like she would like to hear the marketing plan so they invited her to come to the Monday Night Success Meeting with Tiffany.

After the party, Chris and Tiffany talked it over and agreed that she should try to work consistently at this for six months and see how it went. They also agreed that the first priority was to pay off the debt on their credit card before spending any of the money she earned.

Each week, Tiffany held appointments on Thursday Evening and Saturday mornings. In addition, she tried to hold at least one "Play Day" selling appointment with Moms from Addison's class that had children Lily's age. At every appointment, Tiffany asked for referrals from each of her guests. At the end of her first month, Tiffany had sold over $1200 in retail product. She reordered the product she had sold and even subtracting gas money and the hostess gifts she had given to her party hostesses, She still had $500 profit to show for her efforts.

Tiffany offered to show the marketing plan to each of the women she gave a facial to or met at a Mary Kay Party. In addition, she invited several guest to each success meeting and rarely missed having a guest at each meeting.

By the end of her second month, Tiffany had sold another $1200 in product and had $500 to show for her effort in profit. Additionally, 2 women had signed up to join her team making her a Senior Consultant. Tiffany received recognition at her Success Meeting for moving up the career path and received a "Love Check" (because we love to get them) from the company for the wholesale orders her new team members submitted. The combined orders totaled $2200 and her 4% commission was $88 so in her second month she made $588 for her efforts.

In her third month selling Mary Kay Tiffany did a little better in sales. She still did the same amount of work but some of her customers had used up their product and reordered. this month she had $1450 in sales - she reordered $725 and had $625 left after expenses. She continued sharing the marketing plan and added 3 more team members. Magic began to happen here starting with the 3rd team member. This propelled her to Star Team Builder and got her special recognition at her weekly success meeting. She got to wear the coveted Red jacket and earn special seating at the meeting. Her commission changed also. At the end of the month, she had 5 on her team and this entitled her to 9% or 13% commission. Once she got to her fourth team member, she was entitled to 9% plus a $50 bonus for any new team member that placed a $600 order in their first or second month in the business.

Once she has 5 team members, she can receive a 13% commission when 5 or more team members order in that month and she does at least a $600 wholesale order herself. Tiffany's team did $2900 in wholesale order this month and she received a 9% commission because only 3 members of her team ordered. All totaled she made $650 in profit from sales, $261 in commission on the wholesale production and a $50 signing bonus (only one did $600 in her first order.) Her total sales commission and bonus for this month is $961.

During the fourth month for Tiffany, she continued to hold appointments, add team members and service her existing customers. She continued over $300 per week in retail product. Her sales are helped by the fact that customers not only reorder products they have used but they also try other things Tiffany recommends to them as she gets more comfortable with her product knowledge. Her customers are recommending her to friends and family and she is offering the opportunity to anyone who will listen. She has five team members and 3 of them are really motivated to be successful. She has a challenge from her sales Director to add 5 team members and "Gold Medal." She also realizes that with 5 team members, she has enough team embers to go "On Target" for the Chevy Cruze. She just needs to increase her monthly production.

By the end of the fourth month, Tiffany added 5 new team members giving her a total of 10. Her combined total production for the month exceeds the required production to go on target for her first Consultant car. Her 5 new team members have done $4000 in wholesale production; her existing team has done $500 and her own $750 order from her $1500 in personal sales and reorders count toward car production. Tiffany's wholesale order can count toward car production but she will not receive a commission on her own order until she is a Director. Her 13% commission on her teams $4400 of wholesale production is $572 plus her $650 in profit from sales and $150 in new team ember bonuses total $1372!!

Three great things happen at the end of her fourth month. She is "On Target" for the use of a Free car - she needs to add 4 more team members over the next 4 months and combined they need to order $15000 more to complete car qualification (I cover this in more depth in the next chapter.) She also has paid off all of her initial credit card loan from her profits and commissions so now she is able to keep that money to help with the bills, save for a vacation or put something aside for Addison and Lily's education. Most exciting, her Director has asked to meet with her and Chris to discuss Tiffany submitting for D.I.Q.

They met again on a Saturday morning to discuss what becoming a "Director In Qualification" entails and what they can expect. Her Sales Director shared that Tiffany has done extremely well and she would be a fabulous leader. Moreover, the company looked for people with integrity like Tiffany and Chris. She explained how the company rewards Sales Directors for promoting the product and developing Consultants and future leaders. She went on to show them how had Tiffany already been a Director, her commission would have been much more. Given the exact same effort, she would still have made her $650 profit from her sales. She still would have received her 13% check but it would also include her $750 order totaling $682 for her 13% on her personal team and another 13% for her Unit production. In addition, there is a Unit Volume Bonus of 10% per $1000 for Total Unit volume over $5000. So all total, as a Director, Tiffany would have received $1865 in commission and bonus on her team's production plus her 5 new qualified personal Team Members would bring her an additional $500. There is also a Unit building bonus for Sales Directors who add at least 3 qualified team members in a month. The bonus is $300 for 3 or 4 qualified new team members or $500 for 5 or more qualified. in this case, Tiffany would have received $100 each for her personal qualified tem members and a $500 bonus for adding to her unit. Counting her profit from sales, she would have made $3490 for doing exactly the same work she was already doing.

Chris and Tiffany became excited and asked what they would need to do to get to this next level. With the help of Tiffany's Sales Director, she submitted for D.I.Q. and they created an action plan. Tiffany's Director explained that since she was already tracking production for Car Qualification, she could use the same basic strategy only she would need to add 13 more team members as Tiffany herself qualifies as one of the 24 it takes to become a Director. They were excited to realize that once Tiffany submitted for D.I.Q, each time one of her team members brought in a team ember, they too would count for her team.

In addition, the team would need to produce $18000, in team production to complete the qualification but that would not be a problem as they were already tracking $20,000 for Car.

Tiffany's Director complimented her on her consistency in ordering each month. She consistently ordered $600 or more earning her prizes in the Company Star Program. In addition, each qualified new team member added $600 to her own Star Category allowing her a higher star prize.

Chris and Tiffany decided that day that he would take on less overtime so she would have at least one additional time slot during the week for selling appointments and team building interviews. Chris admitted to Tiffany and her Director he had been skeptical about the opportunity and Tiffany's ability to be able to juggle her family life and business. He realized that Tiffany learned the skills as she needed them and her Sales Director and Mary Kay girlfriends were there to help her every step of the way. What he was most excited about was the quality time he got to spend with his daughters while Tiffany was enriching the lives of her customers and team members.

I

hope this fictional story has helped you see how the money starts out small but can grow exponentially with consistent effort and staying the course. Once again I want to point out that there is no set time period of success. I have met quite few people that did this much and more in their first month and I have met many that have been in for years and have yet to add their first team member. I have met very few women in this business that did not just absolutely love what they were doing!

The keys to this business are consistency and repetition. The business itself is simple to learn but I am not saying it is easy. To schedule an appointment for a facial, your wife will speak to 3-5 people. Of the appointments she schedules, a percentage will cancel or reschedule. Some of her appointments will result in little or no sales. On the other hand, this is a business built on relationships and over the top customer service. Customers who appreciate exceptional service not only stay customer for life, they refer their friends and family members resulting in a larger customer base and a larger pool of potential team members.

I have no way of knowing your situation. I can tell you that in my own circumstance, had Marsha taken a job working for wages, we would have had to pay for after school day care for our younger children, quite possibly additional transportation to and from school expenses, commuting expenses - you get the picture.

As I have previously mentioned, the person my wife has become and watching the difference she has made in the lives of her customers, and team members is impossible to measure. I can easily measure the progress she has made in terms of financial growth but the things I am most thankful for are impossible to quantify.

8 What About The Cars?

"But my love is bigger than a Honda, it is bigger than a Subaru
Hey man there's only one thing, and one car that will do
Anyway we don't have to drive it, honey, we can park it out in back
And have a party in your pink Cadillac..."
~Bruce Springsteen

I have mentioned the car program earlier but I think this program deserves a chapter of its own. In 1968, Mary Kay purchased a Cadillac Coupe De Ville and had it repainted the distinctive pink at the dealership in Dallas where she purchased it. The car served as a mobile advertisement for the business and inadvertently created one of the most recognized company trademarks in the world. Independent Sales Directors wanted to know how to get theirs. The next year, Mary Kay started the Career Car Program, offering the free use of pink Cadillac Coupe De Villes to her top 5 Sales Directors. That 1970 Coupe De Ville in Pepto Bismol Pink went on to become the most coveted award in the Mary Kay line-up. Tell anyone that your wife is in Mary Kay, and you will be asked "Is she driving a Pink Cadillac?"

The car program is one of the most significant incentives for success in this business. Consultants can go on target to earn the use of a career car when they have added 5 members to their team and as a team has achieved a minimum for the month of $5000 in wholesale ordering. The current Consultant Car is a white or red Chevrolet Cruz. It comes with On-Star Navigation and Sirius-XM Radio as well as Power Windows, AC, remote entry just to name a few of its features. In our model from the previous chapter, we assumed $1200 in personal sales resulting in a $600 restock order. The rest of her 5 team members in this example would need to order $4400 in wholesale orders to begin qualification. They will need to maintain a monthly Minimum of $5000 in monthly wholesale ordering. This team has 4 months to complete qualification however the use of the Career Car is complete when the personal team reaches 14 and collectively the wholesale orders total $20,000. Once qualified, the team will need to continue producing at the $5000 level or above. During the time between completion of the qualification and pick up of your brand new automobile, the wholesale production generated is "banked" in case there is an off month down the road.

When you go to pick up your new vehicle, there will be a party atmosphere at the dealership. Your wife will sign papers saying she received the car and the necessary mileage forms for your state. Mary Kay pays for the majority of the insurance, deducting the Consultants portion from her team commission. Mary Kay also pays all tax, title and license fees. The only out of pocket expense will be fuel and oil changes. There is no limit to how many miles you put on the car during the 2 years you have it. Consultants are encouraged to drive the car everywhere for business and personal use. You will only be able to deduct actual miles used for business so it is wise to purchase a mileage log from an office supply or use a Smart-phone app. It is important to note that only drivers that are listed on the insurance can drive the car. Family members can be added by contacting the company Career Car Services.

As you wife builds her team and becomes a Sales Director, she will be building toward the premier level of Car Qualification and will have several choices in the Car she chooses to drive. The Premier level currently offers a well equipped black Chevrolet Equinox or a Black Toyota Camry. Moving up the path with higher unit production qualifies her for the current premier plus offering of a well equipped Black BMW 320i.

The Prized "Trophy On Wheels" Pearlized Pink Cadillac is currently offered to Directors that reach the required level of Wholesale production for a sporty SRX Crossover. In Cadillac tradition, it is loaded with everything you would expect from a Cadillac and retails at over $40,000. Many men have told me they would not be comfortable driving a pink car but I can tell you, every husband of a Pink Cadillac Director I know drives with Pride! Driving Pink means your wife has not only provided excellent service to her customers, she has also led and equipped a team of ambitious women who have decided to pro-actively help with their family finances. Driving Pink also means your wife is making some serious money with her Mary Kay Business - often six figures. No one will ever stop your wife and ask if she sells insurance when she is driving her pink trophy! If some wise guy ever gives you hard time about driving a pink car, I would ask them what color free car does their wife drive?

Thanks to the Mary Kay Career car program, we have earned the use of free cars for over 12 years. I would estimate that is over $100,00 in car payment s and insurance payments we did not have to pay. The company does offer a cash compensation in lieu of the car should your family circumstance require it. At the current levels, your wife could receive $375 per month for the Consultant car, $500 per month at the Director level of car and $900 for the Cadillac level. Most people choose to take the car as it says Mary Kay on it and it is a symbol of success. If you look over those values however, it does not take long to realize how much you are saving by driving free. Calculate a Consultant level car payment at $375 per month over a space of 4 years and you could fund a college education for a child, make a substantial down payment on a house or take a great vacation every year. Calculate 4 years against the value of driving a Director level car of even better the prestigious Cadillac level and you could fund multiple college educations, put a large down payment on a house or take really awesome vacations each year. Or buy a boat or fund retirement, send kids from church to camp, pay a great tithe each month - you let your imagination explore this phenomenon. I can tell you that in our circumstance, not having a car payment has provided opportunities beyond our expectations.

A few years back we received a brand new Malibu (the Consultant level car a few years ago) and qualified for the equinox before we had put 3000 miles on the Malibu. Mary Kay Career Car Services called and told Marsha they were ordering her Equinox and she would receive it in approximately 90 days. Marsha told them the car we had was still new and barely had 3000 miles on it. They replied that really did not matter - she had earned the higher level car so they were awarding it. What other company would award you the use of a new car after you had only had the previous one a few short months just because you earned it? I know of one young lady who just recently earned and received four levels of car in less than a year. She earned her Chevrolet Cruz as a Consultant, quickly became a Director and earned a Chevrolet Equinox, shortly thereafter she earned the prestigious Mary Kay Black Mustang (previous Premier Plus Car replaced by BMW) and has recently earned and received her Pink Cadillac.

Now this young lady was moving very fast. She is currently earning over $10,000 a month as Mary Kay Sales Director and has promoted several people from her unit to Directorship. Please understand my heart and do not confuse these results with whatever expectation you may have for your wife's Mary Kay journey. Every Consultant has the same opportunity to do well in this company with no limits on how successful or how fast she moves up. This particular Director has moved rapidly through the career car path, proving it is possible. She did it with while raising 6 children! You can bet that during this period of rapid growth, her husband was supporting her by helping with of a lot of things on the home front.

Car maintenance is one of the areas where I can be of great help to Marsha. Each time she has earned the use of a new car with Mary Kay, I have taken the time to wax it within the first few days of bringing it home for the first time. This helps keep that brand new look and it is a simple matter to wash it every week or so and detail it with a little spray wax. I view the Car Program as a gift from God supplied by Mary Kay and try to take care of it as a precious gift from our Lord.

I also try to help with loading and unloading her product and sales aids when she leaves for and returns from a party.

Mary Kay provides many other rewards and recognition of accomplishments. Imagine your wife wearing diamonds and taking you on 5 star vacations all paid for by Mary Kay. Mary Kay recognizes and rewards achievements at every level and offers Cinderella prizes to those that realize their dreams.

9 Being Supportive

It's better to have a partner than go it alone.
Share the work, share the wealth.
And if one falls down, the other helps,
But if there's no one to help, tough!
~ Ecclesiastes 4:9-10 (MSG)

The dictionary gives several definitions of supportive - providing additional help, encouragement, physical and emotional comfort, sympathy or assistance. Being supportive can also imply advocating, voting for, or defending. The word itself can be a noun or adjective. When it comes to being a supportive spouse, most of us find the definition is anything but clear. When your wife asks you to be more supportive, I do not have to tell you it is difficult to play the role of a mind reader in your relationship. It would be so much easier for us as men if they could just come out and say: "this is what I am feeling and here is what I need you to do to help me."

One thing I have learned is that it is easier to ask what Marsha expects from me as opposed to me trying to second guess her. When it comes to supporting your wife in her Mary Kay endeavors, there are quite a few ways to approach it.

From the emotional side, I have learned that when Marsha wants to talk about her business, she really doesn't want my input or my God-given desire to "fix what's broke." What she is really asking me to do is to be a sounding board to share her thoughts and concerns with. She wants me to remind her she can do it - especially when we put it in prayer and trust God as our business partner. She wants to hear that I believe in her success and respect her ideas and decisions. The hardest part of all this for me is the fact that I tend to want to put in my two cents worth and what is desired from me is to listen objectively. The best way I can break this down for you is like this; I am less apt to want to talk about my feelings and more likely to discuss the practicalities and circumstances of my day while Marsha prefers to share the feelings she had while experiencing her day. It doesn't make either of us a bad person but we are stronger as a couple when we realize each others need to communicate and are willing to listen to each other. As men, we are biologically designed to act on extreme emotions rather than discuss them. So when you notice your wife is upset or distracted, it might be a good idea to ask if she wants to discuss it but DO NOT offer advice unless she asks. All she wants from you is to listen and affirm her feelings.

I do look at our Mary Kay business as a serious business. I treat it as though together we had pooled all our resources and opened a McDonald's franchise. As a business, it requires record keeping, strategic planning and constant re-evaluation. I am a big part of Marsha's Goal setting and strategy planning and I treat it like it is our asset and responsibility not just hers. I am not threatened by her success - I am delighted in it. When we add a new team member, realize we reached a new milestone in her commission or pick up a new Mary Kay car, I am grateful to be part of the process. This process has done more to raise Marsha's self esteem, self confidence and self image than I could ever hope to. Do not misunderstand, I am still responsible for encouraging Marsha to be the very best she can be, I am merely stating I find it liberating to allow her the freedom of my encouragement while she pursues her goals and dreams.

I will explore this aspect a little deeper in the next chapter. I believe that your wife will want and need your emotional support as she builds her business. I also believe this business will help you and her grow in many more ways than you can imagine.

From the practical and logistical side, it is much easier to give you insights. If your wife is meeting her clients outside of the home, there is the necessity of transportation. I try to make sure the car is clean, has gas, and is in good running order with license and tags up to date. I generally make a point of loading the car with her sales kit and materials when she is getting dressed for an appointment. If the appointment is in our home which we have learned is most efficient for us, I tidy up around the house, "Hoover" when necessary and clean the kitchen. I also do most of the record keeping and help with the shipping and receiving of product.

I suggest if your are so inclined, get familiar with using a PC or tablet to access www.marykayintouch.com which is the website Consultants use as a dashboard for their business. I also help with processing credit cards and capturing sales information into a customer database to help Marsha remember what products her customers are using.

I highly recommend you start attending some of her success meetings, guest events and by all means go to Seminar. A small percentage of husbands attend Seminar and I promise you will be treated like a rock star for being supportive. I can not begin to tell you how life-changing this annual event can be. When I was still in my corporate job, I saved up vacation days just so I could attend. The training delivered is obviously for Mary Kay Consultants but it so applicable to life, relationships, work and home.

I also recommend career conference and once your wife becomes a Director, Leadership Conference. You just can not imagine what it is like. I could fill these pages with words that would be meaningless against what you will take away from the experience. Suffice it to say that Mary Kay set out to build a company that would empower women to be the very best they can be - spiritually, at home and in their business. Her emphasis was on developing yourself to your fullest potential while maintaining the highest level of integrity. In addition, there will be awesome stories of accomplishment against all odds from those who have reached a high level of success in the company. Most of these women attribute the largest part of their life success to changes only God could have accomplished in their lives. It is both inspirational and moving to be in the presence of such humble greatness!

I strongly recommend you take a little time and read the information the company provides to new Consultants and watch the training DVD that comes in the starter kit. Sit down with your wife and set goals together - for her business and your family. Plan your time out - short term and long range. Plans can and will have to be adjusted but if you have an agreed upon strategy and a prioritized list of things that have to be done, it is so much easier to adjust on the fly.

More than anything else, the most empowering thing you can do to show your love and support is to share with her that regardless of her outcome, you will always love her and believe in her.

10 Encouragement

"My Purpose is that they may be encouraged in heart and united in love."
~*Colossians 2:2*

It is no secret that women and men view things differently. The Bible is very descriptive about how we as husbands should love our wives. As a matter of fact, Paul provides a detailed description in Ephesians 5 verses 25 - 33 of exactly how we need to love our wives because that is what our wife needs and expects from us. Conversely, our wives are merely instructed to respect us as husbands in the latter part of the passage in Ephesians 5:33.

When I first studied this passage, I found it humorous that we need so much instruction about how we should love our wives and they get the simple "respect your man" suggestion. Paul goes into considerable detail on how we should love our wives reminding us that we need to love our wives as Christ loved the church. Christ held back nothing - He gave his life! We are told further to love our wives the way we love our own bodies and lives. We take care of our daily needs - both physical and emotional and we are therefore to spend equal effort seeing to the needs of our wives. In all, 8 verses of detailed instruction and for our wives 1 sentence - Respect your husband. After giving it some prayer and thought however I came to realize that given the way we differ, this instruction is probably wisely stated for our benefit.

It brings to mind a story that was widely circulated on Facebook a while back and still reappears on a fairly regular basis. The young wife is traumatized because her newlywed husband seems absent minded when he halfheartedly kisses her goodbye on his way to work. She goes through all kinds of traumatizing thoughts that he perhaps thinks it was a mistake he married her or maybe that extra 5 pounds she's carrying or maybe her cooking has turned him away. Before you know it she is crying on the phone, talking to her Mom, her best friend - you get the picture. By the time he comes home, she has imagined he spent the day in the arms of his lover instead of working. They are sitting on the couch watching some TV and she is waiting for the Axe to fall and he's thinking - "I wonder why I'm having so much trouble starting my motorcycle these last few days."

We are made differently for a reason and it is a fact that women have a tendency toward emotion and talking through their issues and we guys are all about action. We like to be decisive and "fix" things when what is really expected is a listening ear. Women intuitively have a greater awareness of how to develop a loving relationship. She instinctively knows how to be supportive, encouraging and nurturing. This is why she needs little instruction from Paul in Ephesians on how to love. We men on the other hand do not have this instinctive awareness on how to encourage our wives.

Recently I was in a spouse class at a Mary Kay function and the facilitator, a marriage therapist, asked did we know what women wanted most from us. There was a lot of guessing and I was fortunate to have already researched this portion of this book. Overwhelmingly women seek security as their primary need. What they want from us, is the knowledge that we will sacrificially and selflessly seek to meet her needs before our own. Realizing that, it is evident that we really need to get to know our wives.

How to encourage

In order that we learn how to be encouraging to our wives, we first need to recognize that just like us they are not perfect. Now I would discourage you from creating a list of your wife's imperfections. Furthermore, I would highly recommend that if you happen to be doodling and a list should pop up, you destroy that list before she sees it. Keep in mind that working as an independent Mary Kay Beauty Consultant, your wife will face many rejections from customers and prospects. It is a natural result of the selling/entrepreneur journey. Appointments cancel, customers and friends don't return phone calls, and team members don't do as they say they will. I urge you to help fend off discouragement by reminding her that it is really not about her. Schedules get changed often - remind her that her Doctor does not close his office when someone does not show for an appointment - neither does her hairdresser. They typically overbook appointments. If by chance multiple appointments do end up holding, someone on her team preferably or someone in her unit will cover the appointment and "dovetail" some of the profits to her. When someone says no, they are not rejecting her so much as saying I don't want or need any right now. The closest thing I can think of to compare this to is when the waitress asks would I like a refill on my coffee and I say "no thanks." Very likely, the waitress will move on to the next customer without ever considering she is a failure or that she should quit.

When we sense our wife needs encouragement from us, I suggest first recognizing she is truly in a struggle. Besides being a good listener, we need to remember that she is sharing something heartfelt. We need to be very careful to think through any response we might share. All too often, we tend to try to fix everything. I have found that more often than not my wife just wants me to listen. If I do make a suggestion, I try to make real sure it is a supportive suggestion. Many guys have discouraged their wives from this business by telling them they should quit. I have found that making a suggestion such as that is exactly the wrong thing to say. Saying that basically says we think they are not capable of being successful in this business. I don't think that builds our wives in the way they hope for us to.

I think a better approach is to remain positive and confident in their abilities and their potential in this business. One thing that will help is to point out some of their previous successes both in business and at home.

It might be a good idea to ask if she still sees this opportunity as a benefit. Does she still dream of making it a success. If it is still her dream, then the last thing we want to do is become a dream buster.

One thing you might consider is to point out the goodness you see in her. I'm not just talking about her business savvy. I'm referring to the qualities you see in her as a mother, as a wife, as a friend and as your chief supporter.

Giving encouragement costs us absolutely nothing - a quick pep talk and a few words of affirmation will go a long way in validating her efforts and dreams. The main thing you want to communicate is that you have her back and want to be there for her when it counts. It seems hard at first to take an interest in makeup and cosmetics - it just isn't in our DNA. The business aspects, the customer service, delivery, logistics and counting the money are more in our natural skill set.

We really need to be especially careful when encouraging our wives not to look at past performance and previous discouragements. When we are so close to someone, it is easy to be critical when what is needed is an open dialog of positive reinforcement and reminders of her potential. We need to be sincere in our words for this same reason. Our wives know us better than we can imagine and will surely pick up any flattering condescension. I can promise you that will not be appreciated. Speaking of appreciation, do not expect to be recognized for being encouraging. If we work at being the natural support person in our partner's life, we need to be able to give encouraging support without any special recognition for it.

Words of Affirmation

I am a huge believer in the power of affirmation. I believe that our mind believes exactly what we tell it to believe. If you want your wife to be wonderful, start telling her everyday how wonderful she is. If you want to have a great marriage, start telling her and yourself how great it is to be married to her. You are probably thinking I am suggesting you practice self-hypnosis. I am fine with you calling it that but I prefer to refer to it as positive affirmation.

Many years ago, I realized when people asked me how things were going, they actually tuned me out if I shared my life dramas with them. Instead, I started saying "fabulous" when people asked me how I was. I noticed a short time later that I actually did feel fabulous! People pay attention when you tell them you are doing fabulous - I guess they would like to feel fabulous also. Psychologists try to explain this with neurons and "happy signals" - I really don't get all that. What I do understand is that you can condition your brain to thinking what you want it to.

I believe that when we begin to turn our thinking around when it comes to our wife, family and work relationships, we can choose to pay more attention to the positive side than the negatives. I can promise you that if you want to feel like the luckiest man alive and be with the woman of your dreams, just start saying to anyone who will listen, yourself and her included, "I am luckiest man to be alive because I am married to the woman of my dreams and she loves me."

Encouragement or giving courage to our wife is perhaps one of the most powerful things we can do for them. You are planting seeds for both her future and yours. I realize this book is intended to help you encourage your wife to be her best in business but I think you will agree that these same principles can be applied to every part of your shared lives. I hope you will take some of these thoughts to heart and sincerely hope you find some of this helpful in building a fabulous relationship with your wife.

11 What Can I Do?

*"One only needs two tools in life: WD-40 to make things go, and duct tape to
make them stop."*
~ *G.M. Weilacher*

I have been asked numerous times "so what are some things I can
do to help my wife be more successful in this business?" I have
already covered being supportive and giving encouragement in
previous chapters. I have also mentioned some of the tasks I have
taken on; loading the car for parties, keeping the car clean and safe
and well maintained. In addition, I have learned to track customer
sales and inventory in the computer system we use as well as creating
postcards and flyers for different customer and unit promotions.

I firmly believe in working within your skill set, however the
money side of this business comes from what Marsha does. The
more she can be out meeting people, servicing customers and
building women up to be future leaders in our company, the more we
are moving in a positive direction. For these reasons, I have pushed

myself to learn things about the business, the products and the marketing system. In addition, I have tried to be a resource for the husbands and boyfriends of our unit members and other Mary Kay families.

In previous years, I did a lot of the transporting of our children to and from their activities and helping them with their daily tasks. I look at this time with my family as some of the richest rewards Mary Kay has provided us. I encouraged the kids to take turns helping me plan and prepare meals as well as (reluctantly) helping me with clean-up chores. In my younger years, I missed a lot of these bonding opportunities with my children. I can look back now at the quality time I have been able to spend with my children and grandchildren with the realization that without Mary Kay, I would have missed many of these opportunities.

Over the years, our business has enabled us to have help with housekeeping and lawn care. We are currently investigating hiring someone to maintain our swimming pool. In the early years, I did as many of these tasks as I could so we can enjoy these benefits now and I can assure you it is well worth it. I have heard many men say they could not stand to watch someone else mow their yard or they find it therapeutic. I say more power to them and you if that is your preference but I also would like for you to have that choice. I personally enjoy detailing our cars but could easily afford to hire that done as well - once again, choices are everything!

Making deliveries to customers is one of the chores I am able to do in the process of doing other errands. Marsha makes the delivery whenever she senses an opportunity to sell more products to her customer or to meet prospective customers or team members. A large majority of these deliveries are reorders that come in from her website and often are just a matter or dropping the product off and picking up a check. I run these errands when I am on my way to the bank to make Marsha's deposits and picking up laundry or groceries. Mary Kay fits into my lifestyle in much the same way it works its way into Marsha's - if you are doing life anyway, making money while doing it is sweet!

I also try to help with the communication side of this business. Often when customers or Consultants call, Marsha is busy doing a party or holding a facial. Other times, she is training her team members. I try to keep up with phone messages, texts and emails and try to help her keep these prioritized so no one feels left out. I also try to stay up with the latest tech tools and social media options. I am definitely not an expert but I have learned to watch what other Consultants and Directors do well and if I can't figure out how to do it, I will contact them and ask or watch a YouTube video on a particular technology or skill.

I hope this has helped you see that there are many things you can do to help your wife without having to learn make-up. If you should discover other ways of helping your wife, please let me know so I can pass the ideas along to other men that want to help their wives.

12 No Sex No Supper?

"Tonight it's beer or nothin'...
leave you dishes in the sink"
~ Porky

"Two in a bed warm each other.
Alone, you shiver all night."
~ Ecclesiastes 4:11 (MSG)

One of my favorite National Sales Directors , Jan Thetford has often said that the month of June is "No Sex No Supper" month. June is the final month of the Mary Kay fiscal year and all Seminar recognition is based on performance from July 1 - June 30. I will admit the first time I heard her say this it gave me some concern. I mean maybe I could live a few weeks on fast food and sandwiches... I have also heard National Sales Director Jill Moore say the sexiest thing her handsome husband Brian says to her is "Honey I'm cooking for you tonight, what would you like?"

Seriously, the first time I heard her say this, I decided it might be a good time to brush up on my cooking skills. I found that not only could I help with the cooking, I actually enjoy doing it. I must admit I did not see myself as the family meal planner, preparer or clean up dude when I was growing up. When I first started "helping out" in the kitchen, I realized the very best time for Marsha to catch people at home was when they were just getting home or while they were cooking. She would get involved in talking about products, taking orders or doing customer follow ups. Invariably, something would either get left in the oven too long or miss getting put in the oven. At first, I "hung out" and kept an eye on things but gradually, it grew on me and I started doing the actual cooking, eventually even planning a lot of the meals.

This way my kids and I could eat good food without breaking the bank at restaurants which would have wasted a lot of the good money Marsha was working for.

Over time, the kids developed a liking for some of the things I cooked. My homemade Pan Fried Pizza has been a family favorite. I have also cooked a few things that my kids absolutely detested. A memorable moment came when our youngest was sharing the blessing and he asked God to not let anyone die from eating my Corned Beef and Cabbage.

Part of my purpose in writing this book is to encourage you the reader to help with some of the kitchen duty. Now I know the thought of cooking and working in the kitchen will make some of you pretty nervous. I imagine some of you are saying "Andy I didn't sign on for no cooking class." I am okay with that and I certainly don't want to push the envelope when it comes to your comfort zone. I am merely suggesting you take a look at the simple fun recipes I have included. Who knows, some of them may actually make your mouth water a little. Or maybe after eating at McDonald's and Pizza Hut several times you might want to try something different.

I certainly haven't lost any weight on my cooking and I think Marsha has grown to like some of my creations. As for Jan's description of June, I have decided to stay away from the "No Sex" part of Jan's equation. I might suggest however that with the right culinary prowess, that part will work itself out for you.

I am going to recommend you take stock of your pots and pans and cooking utensils. I would recommend that at a minimum you have access to a Crock Pot, A George Foreman Grill, some pans suitable for baking, a skillet or frying pan and a pot big enough to make soup, or boil pasta. In addition, a few sharp knives, smooth and serrated will come in handy.

Spices and condiments are mostly personal taste but I would recommend you have some of the basics such as Garlic Salt or Powder, Black Pepper (I suggest Peppercorns and a grinder,) Cayenne, Basil, Cumin(ground,) Nutmeg (ground,) Cinnamon (ground and stick,)Red Pepper, Paprika, Onion Powder and Oregano. There are many other spices to choose from and these are just some basic staples for ordinary "Man" Cooking. I also recommend having some of your favorite seasonings on hand; Steak + Fajita Seasoning, Poultry + Fish Seasoning, Worcestershire Sauce, Teriyaki, Louisiana Hot Sauce, Ketchup, Mayo and Mustard. I cook a lot with Extra Virgin Olive Oil. I also keep plenty of beef stock, chicken Stock, Canned Diced Tomatoes and Cream of Mushroom Soup in the pantry. I also like to keep some Sesame Oil and Rice Vinegar on hand for their flavoring. I also buy the packets of Fajita seasoning, Buttermilk Ranch Dressing and various gravy flavorings.

I am not suggesting you go out and buy everything you don't have. Buy it as you need it and here's a hint - don't buy large sizes in spices. They lose there flavor over time. Jesus said in Matthew 5:13"...if salt has become tasteless, how can it be made salty again? It is no longer good for anything except to be thrown out and trampled under foot by men." Luke had an even more interesting take on the words of our Lord in chapter 14 verses 34-35 "Salt is good but if it loses it's saltiness, how can it be made salty again? It is fit neither for the soil nor the manure pile; it is thrown out." Remember also, with spices and seasoning, a little bit will go a long way.

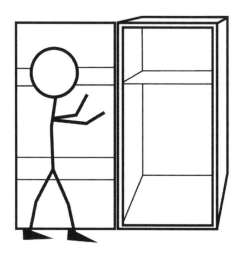

13 What's For Supper?

Homemade Pan Pizza

"You better cut the pizza in four pieces because I am not hungry enough to eat six."
~ *Yogi Berra*

I have always enjoyed pizza and appreciate the ease in which I can call the local pizza delivery service and have a couple of pies delivered to my house. Typically, 2 medium pizzas delivered will set me back about 25 bucks.

The reason I make my Homemade Pan Fried Pizza has nothing to do with saving money even though it is less than half the price of delivery. It is more about really great taste and made to order on the spot for whoever is eating it. I buy frozen Bread Dough at the grocery. On days when I know I am making the Pizzas, I spray a large mixing bowl with Pam (any cooking spray will work or use a vegetable oil spread lightly with a paper towel,) place a couple of frozen loaves in the bowl and cover with a wet dishtowel. I do this first thing in the morning so when I am ready to cook supper, the dough has defrosted and risen.

Next I heat up spaghetti sauce. To save time, I purchase it in the jar but I have also made my own from simmering tomato sauce with tomato paste and various herbs and spices. You want to cook this on the stove because it needs to be as hot as you can get it without bubbling over. It is the heat from the sauce that melts the cheese. I take a handful of dough, roll it into a ball and flatten it out. You can use a rolling pin and flour to spread it out but I find it is just as easy to stretch it out by just pulling it out with my hands. The idea is to make it just a little smaller than your frying pan. You will need a tiny bit of oil - Olive oil works fine. Melted butter will work as will non stick spray. I place the dough in the lightly oiled pan and cook it till the bottom starts to brown. As Soon as I flip it, I put a layer of grated mozzarella on the cooked side and add some of the piping hot sauce over the cheese to melt it. I usually cook a variety of meats, a little hamburger, Italian sausage and pepperoni and sautéed onions and peppers beforehand, I add meat and veggies by individual request, top with a little more sauce followed by some more cheese. The Pizza is done when the bottom has begun to brown. These Individual Pizzas are guaranteed to please and they are easy to make.

Crab Cakes

"If a D.C. Event doesn't have crab cakes, You better flee"
~ Tony Hale

As much as I love the beach, I am not currently near any body of water that yields crabs. Marsha and I absolutely love crab meat and often split an order of Crab cakes as an appetizer when we eat out at a nicer restaurant. In my travels, I came to realize the finest Crab Cakes I have ever had were from Baltimore. I set out to learn how to make them so from time to time I could make them for Marsha when she needed extra culinary encouragement or when we were celebrating or face it whenever we just don't feel like dieting. I am very fortunate to have a Daughter In Law - Alexis who is a superb cook and taught me how to make them. Surprise your wife with some of these Crab Cakes and she no telling how much she will brag on you to her girl friends.

You'll need a can of Jumbo Lump Crab meat or if you are lucky enough to buy it fresh, get about a pound. I buy it canned. It is sold refrigerated and has a sweetness to it that is just perfect.

I am not big on measuring but I would guess about 4 tablespoons of Mayonnaise mixed with a large egg a little Worcestershire sauce (1/2 teaspoon) a teaspoon of mustard, a teaspoon of fish seasoning such as Old Bay seasoning, a teaspoon of lemon and a 1/4 teaspoon of salt.

Drain the crab meat and check for shells and set it aside. Mix everything else together in a small bowl and combine loosely with the crab meat but avoid mashing it. Mix in some fresh breadcrumbs from soft white sandwich bread. A little fresh parsley sprinkled into the mix adds to the look and taste. Once again, mix thoroughly but gently. Cover with plastic wrap and let it sit in refrigerator a few hours. When you are ready to cook and serve, shape the mixture into hamburger shaped cakes - you should get 6 to 8. Heat a few tablespoons of butter with olive oil in a skillet. When the butter is melted, place the cakes in the pan and cook until the underside is brown - about 3-4 minutes on medium heat - flip and cook the other side until browned. My mouth is watering now just thinking about it - but wait; Crab cakes need sauce. Baltimore style sauce is basically a mixture of Mayonnaise, old bay seasoning and lemon juice with perhaps a little garlic and onion powder to boot. If you are like me and have a little bit of the "south" in you, you probably will want a Remoulade style sauce. Start out with some mayo, maybe a cup, 1/3 cup Ketchup (I'm just guessing here, you gotta work by taste,) add a little horseradish or hot mustard or both, some garlic, paprika and or Tabasco to flavor. Start with a little as you add them together and figure out which tastes suit you.

Fish Tacos

"Give a man a fish and you feed him for a day. Teach a man to fish and you feed him for a lifetime."
~ *Chinese Proverb*

I absolutely love to eat Fish Tacos. If I eat at a Mexican Restaurant and it's on their menu, that is what I order. They are quick and easy to make and everyone who has tried them has told me they love them.

Start with a hot skillet and about a tablespoon or less pure virgin olive oil. My preference is frozen Tilapia loins because I can make them up when the urge strikes as opposed to shopping for fresh fish. There is not much in the way of fresh fish here in Dallas TX other then Catfish. You could probably make Catfish Tacos the same way - I just like Tilapia for its mild flavor and it has a Nice texture when cooked. Any white fish will do. I have also made this recipe with Mahi Mahi. I place the fillets in the heated pan with a small amount of olive oil and lightly season it with Ground Cumin and Fajita seasoning. I buy the envelopes of Taco Bell Fajita seasoning and I try to keep a few on hand at all times. Other brands will work. I have tried Taco seasoning but I prefer the more subtle taste of the Fajita seasoning. I place about a Teaspoon of the Fajita seasoning on the top of each fillet while they are cooking and the ground Cumin as if I were salting the meat. I squeeze a lime over the fish while it is cooking. I flip it when the bottom is white and repeat the seasoning on the bottom side of the Fillets which are now on top. Basically I cook it covered medium high and flip it till it starts breaking up in chunks. I make homemade Guacamole by mashing up a fresh avocado with about a tablespoon of bottled Picante or Salsa. I could probably make a great Salsa or Pico De Gallo but that would add to my cooking time. I serve the Fish tacos on Corn or Flour Tortillas with grated cheese, Slaw, Sour Cream and Guacamole and Picante or Salsa.

Chicken or Steak Fajitas

"The only time to eat diet food is while you're waiting for the steak to cook."
~ Julia Child

One of recipes that all of my kids and Marsha really enjoy is my Fajitas. Typically I buy extra Steak or Chicken when I am grilling so I will have meat for Fajitas but I have been known to fire up my grill up and cook a steak or a few chicken breasts just for Fajitas. More often than not, if I decide to make some up last minute, I will throw a few Frozen Chicken Breasts in the George Foreman Grill. It only takes a few minutes to cook up the chicken that way. Regardless of how you come by your chicken or steak, you will want to slice it fairly thin. A word of caution, if you are dealing with raw meat, keep the chicken and steak separated to avoid serious illness. If I am cooking steak and chicken fajitas, I use two separate pans to be on the safe side. I start out heating my skillet with about a tablespoon of Olive Oil. I peel and slice a few onions - white is my preference but yellow works. I find that about 1/4 to 1/2 inch slices work best to cook them quickly. If the onions are large, I'll cook 2-3. I will cook 4 or 5 if they are Small. Once they start becoming translucent, I add half an envelope of Fajita Seasoning. As I have mentioned elsewhere, My preference is the Taco Bell brand but I have used others and they came out fine. I have also used bottled Fajita seasoning which came out good also. I just find it real convenient to have the envelopes of seasoning on hand in my pantry. As the onions are cooking, I cut Bell Peppers into 1/4 to 1/2 inch slices. Marsha is not crazy about peppers, so I generally will only use 2 medium sized peppers. You can also use red, yellow or orange peppers in place of or along with the green ones. I don't think it changes the flavor so much as makes it more colorful. Once the peppers start cooking, I add in the sliced meet and the rest of the Fajita Seasoning. I squeeze 2- 4 small limes or 1-2 large limes over the entire mix. Here is an Andy trick: Microwave the limes for 15-20 seconds before you cut them. It seems to release the juice easier. I stir the mix several times and I like to add some fresh Cilantro leaves. I tear the leaves from the stems. A lot of the flavor is in the stem but I prefer just using the leaves. I pound the leaves with a heavy sharp knife which brings some of the flavor out. I serve My Fajitas with my homemade Guacamole (see fish Tacos for Guacamole recipe,) shredded cheese, Sour Cream and picante or salsa. Sometimes I'll heat up a can of Refried Beans with a tablespoon of picante and about 1/2 cup of grated cheese and offer that up as well. I think you are beginning to see why I have grown a few sizes over the years.

Crockpot Recipes

I was 32 when I started cooking; up until then, I just ate

~ Julia Child

Someday, I will write a book on Crock Pot Recipes. Actually I probably won't. I will share a few things I have figured out how to do with my Crockpot in the hope that it may help you out a little bit. I have found that just about anything you want to cook up will work in the Crockpot and it has the added benefit of doing the cooking while you are doing something else.

Scalloped Potatoes

One of Marsha's comfort foods is cream of Potato soup. Now I am not crazy about Potato soup so if she is not feeling well, more often than not I will dig out a can of Campbell's Cream of Potato Soup and make a few Grilled Cheese Sandwiches and I am the hero. Sometimes given her appreciation for the potato, I slice a few Potatoes up and toss them in the Crockpot with some bacon or ham diced up, a cup or two of Chicken Broth and a can of Campbell's Cream of Mushroom Soup. I set the Crockpot to medium temperature and let it cook 5 or 6 hours. When we are almost ready to eat it, I'll add a cup or two of grated cheese and voila - scalloped potatoes.

Pork or Pot Roast

I generally prefer The loin portion for its tenderness but the slow cooking will make even the toughest meat tender. I add a can of Cream of Mushroom Soup (you can use the dry mix envelopes of gravy also) I add Coca Cola or Dr Pepper - a couple of cups will do. If you can cook it 8 hours or so, cook it on Low - if you only have 5 or 6 hours, cook it on High. Feel Free to cut up a few Potatoes, carrots and onions if you want it to be more like a stew. Just before serving, you might want to pour off some of the juice and mix in some Gravy flour or cornstarch. Mix it until smooth and pour it back into the pot. Mix and cook on high until it is the consistency you like.

Tortilla Soup

"Only the pure in heart can make a good soup"
~ *Ludwig Van Beethoven*

Throw 4 boneless skinless chicken breasts in the Crockpot with a couple of cans of chicken Broth, an envelope of Fajita Seasoning (I think I have mentioned I like the Taco Bell Seasoning,) A packet of Ranch Dressing Mix a can of corn, a can of black beans, a small can of Ro-Tel, 2-3 diced green onions and some Cilantro leaves. If you have lots of time, cook it on low - if not cook on high. A few hours later, the Chicken should be thoroughly cooked. Cut into small pieces or shred and return to the soup. Cut up some corn or flour tortillas and add them to the mix. Stir regularly, the soup will thicken as the tortillas melt. I serve it with crushed tortilla chips, grated cheese, and sour cream.

Pork Chops and Sweet Potatoes

One of the great cooking tools I have discovered is the parchment bag. I coat some boneless Pork chops with my favorite barbecue rub and place them in a parchment bag with cut up sweet Potatoes and an onion cut in wedges. I add some Ground Cumin and Garlic Salt and cook for 45 minutes to an hour. The Parchment cooking bags are stocked in the grocery store where the aluminum foil and wax paper is and I have found it to be excellent for retaining flavor and keeping meat tender. I finish off the Pork Chops, Sweet Potatoes and Onions off on the Grill outside to brown it a little. The Parchment bags work well with Chicken also. Whenever I cook Chicken or Pork on the grill, I preheat the meat up in the oven at 350 for 45 minutes to an hour to kill off harmful germs. I finish the meat off on the grill about the same amount of time I would cook a steak and have found that precooking Chicken and Pork in the oven tends to keep it from dying out on the grill.

Baked Bread Sandwiches

I cook these when we are having a lot of guests or when a friend or neighbor has a lot of relatives over because someone is sick or has passed away. I buy frozen bread dough just like we used in the Pan Pizza recipe. I thaw the bread and place it in a lightly oiled bowl (large) to rise. I place a damp towel over the bowl to keep the dough from drying out. Once it is risen, I roll the loaf flat until it is 1/4 to 1/2 inch thick all over and about the size of a cookie sheet. With the dough on a slightly greased cookie sheet, I layer thin deli meats and cheeses and whatever dressing suits the meat. If I am using pepperoni, I use Mozzarella cheese and marinara sauce. I use horseradish or perhaps Honey Dijon Mustard on ham or roast beef - it is really a matter of taste. I roll the bread and meat up lengthwise and pour a little melted butter over the top of the roll-up. Bake in the oven at 350 until golden brown. I slice the bead 3/4 of the way through in 1 slices and wrap the roll in foil. I leave the foil wrapped rolls in a warm oven until ready to serve.

Breakfast Casserole

When we have overnight guests during the holidays or an early morning Mary Kay meeting, I brown some ground breakfast sausage in a pan. Once it is cooked, I drain the oil and spread the ground sausage over the bottom of a Pyrex cooking pan. I sprinkle frozen hash browns over the sausage and pour egg beaters over the potatoes. Top it off with some grated cheese and cook at 350 until the eggs are completely cooked.

French Toast

One of Marsha's favorite breakfast foods is French Toast. I have experimented a lot and found that if you toast the bread in the toaster before dipping it in either egg beaters or a few beaten eggs, it has a little more body to it and doesn't get as soggy while cooking. I sprinkle Cinnamon on both sides before coking and top mine off with a little powdered sugar after it is cooked.

Chicken Spaghetti

This was a weekly favorite when all seven kids were home or some of them invited friends, Boil boneless, skinless Chicken Breasts in a pan of water. When meat is white all the way through, remove and cut into small pieces. Save the water from boiling the chicken to boil the spaghetti. When spaghetti is desired consistency, drain and mix with Chicken and Canned Cream Of Mushroom Soup. Add in chopped Celery and Onion if desired. Top with grated Cheddar Cheese and bake at 350 about 30 minutes.

Stir Fry

"Everything you see I owe to spaghetti."
~Sophia Loren

I start out by slicing Polish Kielbasa or Turkey sausage in 1/2 inch slices and placing in a medium hot skillet. While the meat is cooking, I start a pot of water on to boil to cook pasta in. I add in chopped or finely cut carrots and green onions. I really don't measure - 3 or 4 green onions, a dozen or so baby carrots. I also add in about a dozen cherry tomatoes or a small package of sun dried tomatoes. I add sliced mushrooms and fresh spinach. I cook pasta - my preference is angel hair pasta or thin spaghetti but bow ties, flat noodle, ramen all work well. Mix it all together in the skillet and add in about a 1/2 cup each of grated parmesan and Feta Cheese and serve. If you need to moisten it up a little, use the water from the pasta - the starch in it will thicken up like a sauce when you mix it all together.

I hope you find a few of these recipes helpful and enjoy trying then out. I left out most of my grilling and barbecue recipes assuming most men are comfortable cooking outdoors on the grill and probably could teach me quite a bit. May you never go hungry in June my friend!

14 Moving On And Growth

On Silver Wings

I have a premonition that soars on silver wings.
It is a dream of your accomplishments of many wondrous things.
I do not know beneath which sky
Or where you'll challenge fate
I only know it will be High
I only know it will be Great!
~ Anonymous

Mary Kay is often quoted as saying " You can do this business with a man or without a man but not against a man." I have personally witnessed the prophetic wisdom of her words. Many of the women experiencing extreme success in Mary Kay have husbands that are supportive and encouraging of their wives and her

Mary Kay team. Conversely, many of the women I have met that seem to struggle share a desire for their husband to be more supportive. This idea for this book is the result of some of the conversations shared with those women.

In talking with some of these men, I have heard a whole myriad of reasons why they are not supportive of their wives. In some cases, they feel like I once did - "there is no way you can make a living selling lipstick." Many times, sharing the concept of Mary Kay's marketing plan and explaining that parties are the mainstay of a successful Mary Kay endeavor has encouraged them to realize the wisdom of helping their wife succeed. I have heard of a few men that have told their wives they have to go out and find a real job. I can testify in watching Marsha and her team at work, this is real work and if done consistently and with diligence, it makes real big girl pay. Think of it like this, if your wife is working in a business where she spends an hour booking appointments for her boss, an hour on customer relations, an hour or two showing a prospective client her companies products and an hour interviewing prospective employees - is that real work? The beauty of her working the Mary Kay marketing plan is that she is working with women in a company that designed its marketing plan around women. Mary Kay believed that every woman should have the opportunity to make executive pay working the hours she chooses so she can be home when her family needs her to be.

In other instances, I have sensed rather than heard a reluctance based on beliefs that the man should be the major bread winner and provider for the family. In addition, there are some men who believe the biblical role designed for men is one of family leadership. I am a strong proponent of biblical belief and can quote you many scriptures in support of this.

Scripture, on the other hand, also references God's intention of a wife being a man's helpmate. A helpmate according to dictionary.com is a companion and helper, a spouse or anything that aids or assists, especially regularly. This definition could describe the GPS on my phone. By digging deeper, the actual words God uses in Genesis 2:18 according to the King James Version is "help meet." The original Hebrew translation implies a "helper" of much deeper significance. The same word for helper is used to describe military alliances and God himself. Literally translated, the original Hebrew says something more like one who surrounds, protects, aids and supports and makes no distinction as to who is in authority.

I am no bible scholar although I do study it on a daily basis. I am comfortable in the assumption that God intended men and women to have an equal role in the procurement of resources.

I also believe that God did intend for men to be the spiritual leaders in our families. That is not to say that a woman cannot fill the role if her man is unwilling or unable. What it does imply is that when we are married, we are responsible one to the other for making sure our spouse is the best he or she can be before God.

The Bible also makes it clear in Proverbs 31 that God does in fact bless women in the business world. This last chapter of Proverbs shows what mature wisdom looks like: it is industrious, responsible and community-oriented. It further instructs us as men to call your wife blessed and praise her. What would it cost you to tell her she is absolutely the greatest woman on earth? Let her know how much it means to you that she cares enough for you and your family to work as diligently as she has. Proverbs 18:22 states the positive side of Genesis 2:18 - it is good for a man to have a good wife. Proverbs 19:14 drives this idea home: "Houses and wealth are inherited from parents, but a prudent wife is from the Lord." Clearly these words are meant to remind us what a treasure we have in our wives and blessed we are that they our ours!

Many read the Proverbs 31 text as an instruction for women to stay home and bake casseroles for her husband while watching the kids. In actuality, the scripture describes what we would today view as an owner of a textile business that invests successfully in real estate. The text is really a description of God's desire for both men and women to put God first, then family and then business. This is the exact principle that Mary Kay taught and is still alive and well in Mary Kay culture today.

I am not here to try and change your marriage or your life. I am trying to show you how it is possible for your wife to have a successful career in Mary Kay yet still fully respect your role as leader of your household. The very worst that could happen is she makes so much money, it no longer makes sense for you to go out and work everyday. I can assure you that in our household this has been our experience and we are truly blessed by it. In addition, our children have learned the positive values that come from running a home based business that encourages keeping biblical principles as the key ingredient to success.

I sincerely hope this short book has been of help to you. I hope and pray for your family and your marriage. I fully believe a Mary Kay business is truly a blessing form God and hope you find this to be the case also. I hope we meet at a Mary Kay Seminar or Leadership Conference and share some great stories of Mary Kay successes in our families. Best of luck and God bless you!

About the Author

"Writing a book is a horrible, exhausting struggle, like a long bout of some painful illness. One would never undertake such a thing if one were not driven on by some demon whom one can neither resist nor understand."
~George Orwell

Andy Stirrat lives in Glenn Heights TX with his beautiful wife Marsha. Together they encourage others to believe *"Dreams Do Come True!"*

Available Fall 2014

Andy's current project - follow www.andystirrat.com for an upcoming free sample chapter!

Wall Builders
Becoming The Leader God Can Use

Made in the USA
San Bernardino, CA
24 April 2015